JOE LOUIS

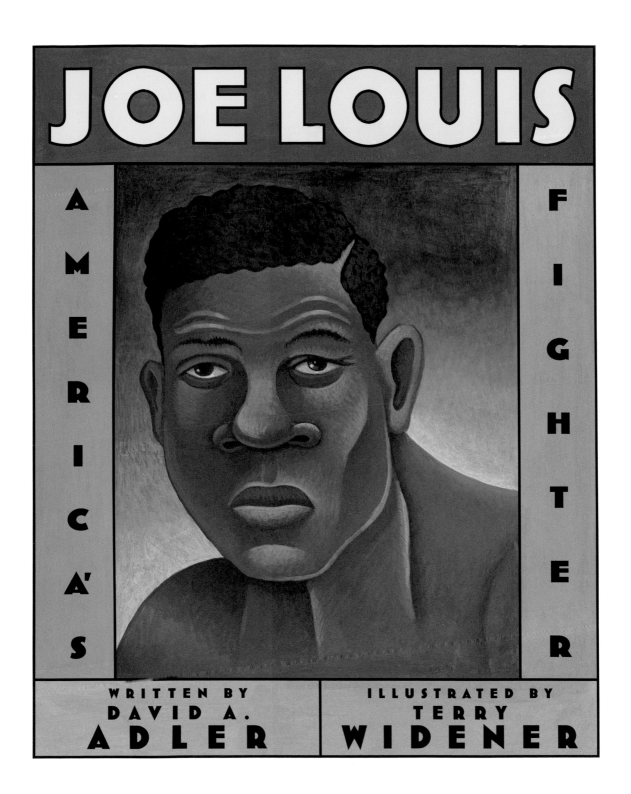

AMERICA'S FIGHTER

WRITTEN BY
DAVID A.
ADLER

ILLUSTRATED BY
TERRY
WIDENER

GULLIVER BOOKS  HARCOURT, INC.

Orlando   Austin   New York   San Diego   Toronto   London

JOSEPH LOUIS BARROW, the grandson of slaves, was born on May 13, 1914, into what he called a "no-place-to-go" world. He was the seventh of Munroe and Lillie Barrow's eight children.

Joseph's family lived in a crowded four-room farmhouse with no electricity or running water. His father struggled to feed and clothe his family. He worked from daybreak to darkness, planting and picking cotton. It was all too much for him. In 1916, Munroe Barrow was taken to the Searcy State Hospital for the Colored Insane. He lived there the rest of his life.

Joseph's mother remarried, and in 1926, she and her second husband moved the family to Detroit, Michigan.

Detroit was a whole new world for twelve-year-old Joseph. The sidewalks and streets were busy with people, cars, and trolleys. His school in Alabama had been only for blacks. In Detroit, he went to a school for black *and* white children.

Joseph worked hard after school at a vegetable market. He delivered ice, too, in a horse-drawn carriage. When he had the time, he and his friends played at boxing.

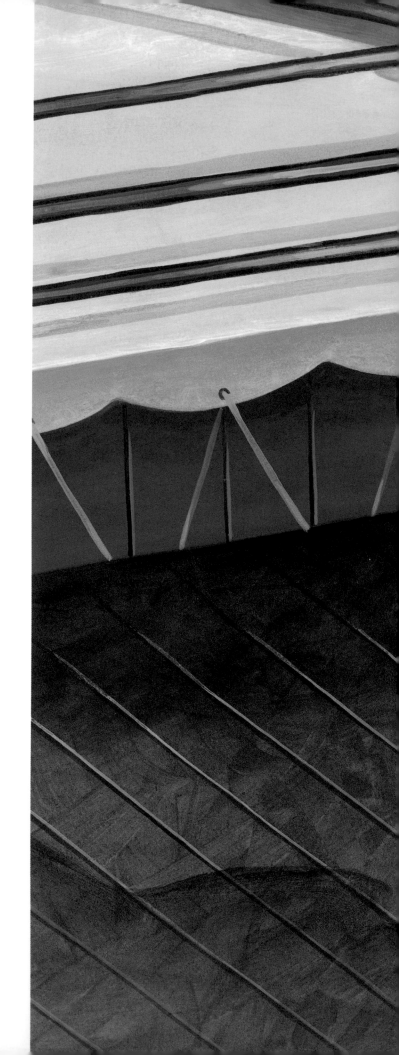

One day, when Joseph was seventeen, his friend Thurston McKinney took him to Brewster's East Side Gymnasium, to see some *real* boxers.

At Brewster's, Joseph fought Thurston and knocked him down. "It was like power pumping through me," Joseph said. He knew then that he wanted to be a boxer.

Joseph quit school in 1932. Later that year, he had his first real amateur fight, a three-round match. When he signed up for the fight, he wrote *Joe Louis* so large, there was no room on the form for *Barrow*. From then on, Joseph Louis Barrow was known as Joe Louis.

That first amateur fight was against Johnny Miler,
a member of the Olympic boxing team. Miler knocked
Joe down seven times and won. Joe's face was cut and
bloodied. His mother cried when she saw him. She told
him to quit boxing.

Joe stayed away from the gym for a few months, but he loved boxing too much to give it up. He went back, determined to become a better boxer, to not lose again. He practiced hard and won his next fourteen fights. He won fifty of his fifty-four fights as an amateur.

On July 4, 1934, twenty-year-old Joe Louis had his first professional fight. It was big-time boxing, with a paycheck. The fight was set to last ten rounds, but Louis knocked Jack Kracken out in the first round!

Joe Louis won all twelve of his fights in 1934, and African American fight fans began to take notice of him. They said he was a "punching machine" and nicknamed him the "Brown Bomber."

The 1930s, the years of the Great Depression, were hard times for most Americans, especially African Americans. Millions of African Americans had lost their jobs. But they still had Joe Louis. They hung his picture in their homes and shops. And when he fought, they found a radio somewhere so they could cheer for their hero.

Most white fans wouldn't root for a black boxer, and some white boxers refused to even fight blacks. Therefore, the match between Joe and Primo Carnera, on June 25, 1935, aroused real interest. Carnera was white and a former heavyweight champion. The match was to be held in New York's Yankee Stadium, just outside of Harlem, an almost all black section of the city.

Some people thought there would be problems in the stadium between black and white fans, and race riots in the city. The police commissioner sent more than a thousand police to Yankee Stadium.

The ring announcer was worried, too. Before the fight, he implored the sixty thousand fans. "Regardless of race, creed, or color, let us all say, may the better man emerge victorious."

Carnera was much taller and heavier than Joe Louis, but Louis got in close and punched. In the sixth round, Louis knocked Carnera down. When Carnera got up, Louis knocked him down again.

This time, Carnera got up slowly, and the referee ended the fight. Joe Louis had won.

In Harlem that night, and in other African American neighborhoods, there were great celebrations.

Three months later, Joe Louis married Marva Trotter, a smart and beautiful young woman from Chicago. On their wedding night, they went to Yankee Stadium. Marva sat ringside as the announcer introduced Joe as "the new sensational pugilistic product, although colored . . . the idol of his people." The fight was against Max Baer, a former heavyweight champion.

In the first round, Louis landed a powerful punch to Baer's jaw. In the second, Louis punched and bloodied Baer's nose and mouth. In the third, Louis knocked Baer down twice. Then, in the fourth, Louis knocked him out.

Joe Louis's mostly black fans celebrated again.

On June 19, 1936, Joe Louis was scheduled to fight another former world heavyweight champion, the German fighter Max Schmeling.

In America, Nazi Germany was already known to be a terror-filled, hate-filled place. In the coming years, the Nazis would torture and kill millions of people because of their race and religion. For many Americans, Max Schmeling was a symbol of that evil regime.

Suddenly, this fight wasn't a black fighter against a white one. It was an American against a German. For many people, both blacks *and* whites, Joe Louis was fighting their fight.

For the first three rounds, Joe Louis put up a strong fight. But in the fourth, Schmeling knocked him down. After that, the fight was all Schmeling's. In the twelfth round, Louis fell to the canvas and was counted out.

Joe Louis was carried to his corner. This was his first loss as a professional fighter and he wept. "It seemed at that moment I would just die," he later wrote. His fans cried, too.

In Germany, Schmeling's fans celebrated. "I know you fought for Germany," one Nazi leader cabled Schmeling. Adolf Hitler, the ruler of Nazi Germany, also congratulated him, and sent flowers to Schmeling's wife.

Joe Louis was very discouraged, but he kept fighting. He won his next eleven fights.

Then, on June 22, 1937, in a huge Chicago stadium, Joe Louis faced James J. Braddock, the world heavyweight champion.

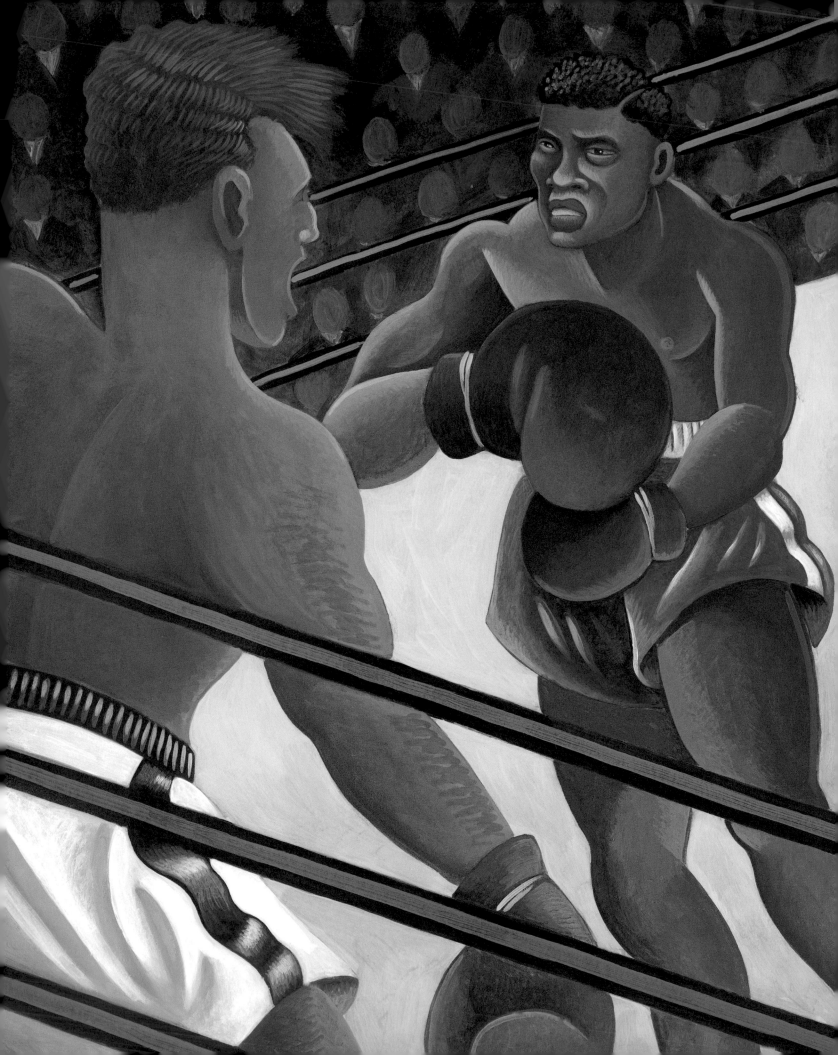

For the first few rounds, the two fighters traded punches. In the sixth and seventh rounds, Louis hit Braddock hard, again and again. Then, in the eighth round, Louis threw a powerful right to Braddock's jaw. The champion fell. He was counted out and carried to his corner.

The stadium crowd cheered. Now there was a new world heavyweight champion, twenty-three-year-old Joe Louis.

In cities throughout the United States, African Americans cheered from open windows. Taxicab drivers tooted their horns. More than ten thousand fans paraded through the streets of Harlem. Their hero was now the world champion!

But in Germany, the press declared that the true champion was still Max Schmeling. Joe Louis was determined to prove them wrong.

On June 22, 1938, with Europe on the brink of war, Joe Louis at last had a rematch with Max Schmeling.

"This isn't just one man against another," Joe Louis said before the fight. "It is the good old U.S.A. versus Germany."

That night, anti-Nazi demonstrators shouted outside New York's Yankee Stadium. Inside, more than seventy thousand fight fans waited to see what Louis would do against Schmeling.

The fight was broadcast in four languages over 146 radio stations. President Franklin Delano Roosevelt, a Joe Louis fan, surely listened. It was reported that Nazi leader Adolf Hitler listened, too, at his mountaintop retreat.

When Joe Louis walked toward the ring, American fans cheered wildly. Some cheered, too, when Schmeling walked out. Others jeered and threw banana peels and paper cups at the German fighter.

The bell rang and Louis came out quickly. He kept
punching, almost without stop. Schmeling countered just
twice, then he fell against the ropes. Louis threw a right
to his jaw, and Schmeling fell to the canvas. Schmeling
got up at the count of three, shaky, almost helpless.
Another punch to the jaw and he fell again. A left to the
chin, and Schmeling fell a third time. He was out!

In just 124 seconds, Joe Louis had beaten Max Schmeling. "*Now* I feel like the champion," Joe Louis said after the fight.

Both black and white Americans everywhere celebrated. Joe Louis was their hero.

"The decline of Nazi prestige," one reporter wrote, "began with a left hook."

Soon after that, the Axis Powers led by Germany were at war with the Allies, led first by England and later by the United States. Joe Louis joined the army. "We can't lose," he said, "because we're on God's side." Seeing Joe Louis in an army uniform, ready to fight for his country, raised America's spirits.

Joe Louis had two title fights while he was in the army. He won them both and gave all the earnings to the Navy and Army Relief Funds. After the war, he continued his fight career.

Joe Louis had twenty-five championship fights and won every one. Before each fight, Louis said he knew that one day "some guy would come along and take the title away from me, but not this guy, never tonight."

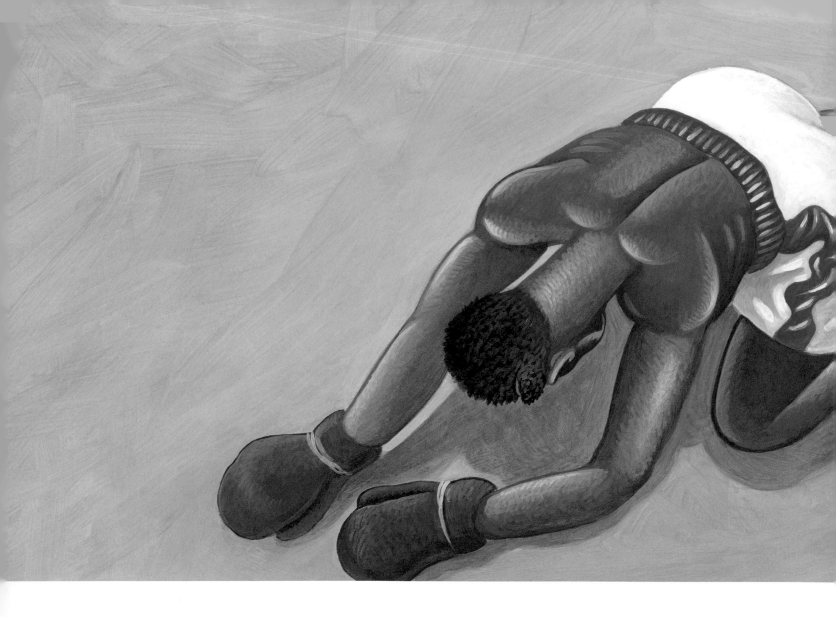

In 1949, Joe Louis retired from boxing, undefeated as world champion.

In 1950, he was back. At thirty-six, he was old to be a fighter, but he missed the excitement of the ring. He wanted to be a champion again. He fought against Ezzard Charles, the new champion, but lost.

He won his next eight fights, but in October 1951, he lost again, to Rocky Marciano. "The record books will say it was Marciano who beat Joe," one reporter wrote, "but everybody knows it was age."

At thirty-seven, Joe Louis retired again—this time for good.

For the next thirty years, until he died on April 12, 1981, people everywhere wanted to meet the great Joe Louis.

In the tough years of the 1930s, when African Americans needed a hero, they had Joe Louis. During the tough years of World War II, when *all* Americans needed a hero, *they* had Joe Louis, too. Many fight fans, black and white, said Joe Louis was the greatest heavyweight champion ever.

AUTHOR'S NOTES

★ Joe Louis's grandmother was an American Indian, but Louis said, "I'm mostly black and I'm proud of that."

★ Joe Louis was married four times, twice to Marva Trotter, and once each to Rose Morgan and Martha Malone Jefferson. He and Marva Trotter had two children, Jacqueline and Joseph, Jr.

★ Joe Louis was the second African American heavyweight champion. The first was Jack Johnson, who knocked out champion Tommy Burns on December 26, 1908, in Sydney, Australia. In July of 1910, there were race riots after Johnson beat the white former champion, Jim Jeffries. When Jack Johnson was champion, white Americans were desperate for a "Great White Hope," a white man to take back the crown. In 1915, the white fighter Jess Willard did.

★ The jungle and animal images used in 1930s newspaper reports of Louis's fights make clear the horrible anti-black sentiments of the time.

★ While Joe Louis was training for the second Schmeling fight, he met President Franklin D. Roosevelt. The president felt Louis's arms and said, "Joe, we're depending on those muscles for America."

★ After the war, it was reported that from a wartime desk job, Schmeling saved children from the Nazis. He and Louis later became friends.

★ When Joe Louis died, a *New York Times* reporter wrote that Louis was "probably the best heavyweight fighter of all time."

Among my sources were two Louis autobiographies, *Joe Louis, My Life* (Harcourt Brace, 1978), written with Edna and Art Rust, Jr., and *My Life Story* (Duell, Sloan and Pearce, 1947); a biography, *Joe Louis: 50 Years an American Hero,* written by his son, Joe Louis Barrow, and Barbara Munder (McGraw-Hill, 1988); and several other biographies, including *Champion—Joe Louis: Black Hero in White America* by Chris Mead (Scribner, 1985) and *Brown Bomber: The Pilgrimage of Joe Louis* by Barney Nagler (World Pub., 1972). I also referred to newspaper accounts of his fights.